GUIDELINES

FOR THE PROFESSIONAL
CONDUCT OF THE CLERGY

GUIDELINES

FOR THE PROFESSIONAL
CONDUCT OF THE CLERGY

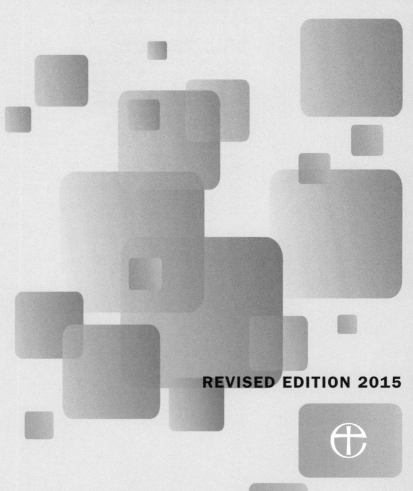

REVISED EDITION 2015

Church House Publishing
Church House
Great Smith Street
London
SW1P 3AZ

ISBN: 978 0 7151 1096 6

Published 2015 by Church House Publishing
for the Convocations of Canterbury and York

Editor: The Reverend Stephen Trott
Typeset by ForDesign
Printed and bound by CPI Group (UK) Ltd, Croydon

contents

Foreword by the Archbishops of Canterbury and York

"In the name of our Lord we bid you remember the greatness of the trust that is now to be committed to your charge."

The solemn reminder about trust that is in the Ordinal confronts all the ordained with the privilege and responsibility entailed in their particular ministry. We know that the Church of God expects high standards, but it also remains true that society at large expects high standards of the clergy. This is true of both those who profess faith in Jesus Christ and those who do not. A failure in meeting the standard expected results in profound disappointment, and a deep sense of being let down.

Yet setting such standards can also be a source for over-anxiety about how we can live up to them.

These *Guidelines for the Professional Conduct of the Clergy* are therefore a source of counsel, advice and comfort. We are all sinners who stand in need of redemption, yet we follow Jesus Christ who brings that redemption. We proclaim the gospel of hope, and are called to underpin all that we do with prayer.

The care of souls and the proclamation of the gospel are demanding roles, but profoundly fulfilling. If we are to be effective we need to take proper care to refresh our learning and to refresh ourselves. There will always be the challenge of getting the balance right, but these guidelines encourage us to do just that.

We remain deeply thankful to God for the faithfulness we see demonstrated so often in the ordained ministry of our Church. Please be assured of our prayers for you. Remember the source of any strength that we find.

"You cannot bear the weight of this calling in your own strength, but only by the grace and power of God. Pray therefore that your heart may be daily enlarged and your understanding of the Scriptures enlightened. Pray earnestly for the gift of the Holy Spirit."

Justin Cantuar:
Sentamu Eboracensis
July 2015

Preface

In 2003 the Convocations of the Provinces of Canterbury and York, representing the bishops and clergy of the Church of England, published a wholly new document, a set of Guidelines describing what is desirable in the professional conduct of ordained ministry. These Guidelines are not a legal code; they are the fruit of shared experience and wisdom offered by clergy to clergy, and to all who share in their ministry, and they are set within an expectation that all the clergy will be familiar with the principles of canon and ecclesiastical law by which their public ministry is governed.

Those who compiled the first Guidelines recognized that a time would come for their revision in response to changes or developments in either the Church or the law of the land. We have welcomed a new Clergy Discipline Measure in 2003; the publication of a new Ordinal in 2007; and in 2009 the new Ecclesiastical Offices (Terms of Service) Measure and Regulations brought reform to many aspects of the ways in which the clergy are deployed and supported. Since 2003 there have also been vitally important changes to the law to ensure the safeguarding of children and vulnerable adults.

The starting point for the Guidelines, both now and originally, is quite rightly the Ordinal, which sets out formally and liturgically the Church's spiritual expectations of its new ministers as they are presented for ordination. The Guidelines are framed, not as a set of detailed regulations, but as an elaboration of the text of the Ordinal. The quotations with which the Guidelines begin, and which appear at the beginning of each section, offer a spiritual and pastoral framework for a lifetime's vocation and ministry as servants of Jesus Christ, deacons, priests and bishops ordained for service and mission in his Church.

The authority which we are given for our ministry is the Holy Spirit, who calls us to consider our vocation and ministry. Through the Church which Jesus Christ founded, this ministry as deacons, priests and bishops is handed on in each generation for his mission in the service of God and his kingdom. Although laws and regulations inevitably play a part in the life of the Church, which must both order its own life and engage with state and society, our calling is primarily spiritual, and we must be guided by the scriptures, by the long experience of the Church which we call tradition, and by the best insights and knowledge available to us in the present age to which our ministry is addressed.

Accordingly a working party was appointed by the House of Clergy of the General Synod, from among the membership of the two Convocations, to revise and update the Guidelines so that they remain available to every ordained minister, and to the Church as a whole, as a valuable resource for reflecting upon our vocation and its exercise in the many spheres of ministry in which clergy are engaged.

The Guidelines are not intended to be a complete compendium covering every aspect of our life and ministry but contain pointers to wider knowledge of other subjects, spiritual, pastoral and legal with which we ought to engage. They are not the last word on any subject, and indeed will be revised at regular intervals in order to keep pace with changes in church and society.

We are very grateful to the Dean of Brechin, the Very Revd Dr Francis Bridger, who has updated for this edition his theological reflection which was originally written for the first edition of the Guidelines in 2003.

Serving in ordained ministry can be a difficult and challenging way of life, with many demands made upon themselves by conscientious clergy as well as by those to whom they minister. We have sought in these revised Guidelines to draw some reasonable boundaries between the sacrificial perceptions of ordained ministry, and the proper need for rest, reflection and care of self and family on the part of those from whom much is asked.

Protection of others forms part of our calling, and it must be applied also to the clergy who serve in a society which is less and less familiar with the Christian tradition of ordained ministry. It is our hope that these Guidelines will also provide useful insights into our training, appointment and deployment for all of those concerned with the ministry of the Church of England.

These Guidelines were approved on 10 July 2015 and declared as an Act of Convocation by the Convocations of Canterbury and York.

The Reverend Stephen Trott
Synodical Secretary of the Convocation of Canterbury

MEMBERSHIP OF THE JOINT CONVOCATIONS WORKING PARTY

The Reverend Canon Moira Astin
The Right Reverend Pete Broadbent
The Reverend Canon David Felix
The Reverend Dr Meg Gilley
The Right Reverend Peter Hill
The Reverend Prebendary David Houlding (Chair)
Mrs Mary Johnston
The Reverend Canon Simon Killwick
The Reverend Stephen Trott (Secretary)

Guidelines for the professional conduct of the clergy

"God calls his people to follow Christ, and forms us into a royal priesthood, a holy nation, to declare the wonderful deeds of him who has called us out of darkness into his marvellous light."

"The Church is the Body of Christ, the people of God and the dwelling-place of the Holy Spirit. In baptism the whole Church is summoned to witness to God's love and to work for the coming of his kingdom."

"To serve this royal priesthood, God has given particular ministries."

"Deacons are ordained so the people of God may be better equipped to make Christ known. Theirs is a life of visible self-giving. Christ is the pattern of their calling and their commission."

"Priests are ordained to lead God's people in the offering of praise and the proclamation of the gospel. They share with the Bishop in the oversight of the Church, delighting in its beauty and rejoicing in its well-being."

Excerpts from the Ordinal
(*Common Worship: Ordination Services 2007*)

The primary aims of these Guidelines are:

- to encourage the clergy – deacons, priests and bishops – to aspire to the highest possible standards of conduct throughout a lifetime of ministry;
- to identify certain basic minimum standards of behaviour;
- to seek to ensure the welfare and the protection of individuals and groups with whom the clergy work, and of the clergy and their families;
- to provide safe and effective boundaries for clerical ministry;
- to encourage personal and corporate ministerial development.

Calling

1   Priests are to set the example of the Good Shepherd always before them as the pattern of their calling.

1.1   The three orders of ordained ministry play a central role in the mission of the Church which Jesus Christ entrusted to his Apostles, to "go and make disciples of all nations, baptizing them in the name of the Father and of the Son and of the Holy Spirit, teaching them to observe all that I have commanded you" (*Matthew 28.19-20*).

1.2   Ordained ministers bear the privilege and responsibility of being servants and leaders in the ministry of the Church. As pastors, spiritual guides and representatives of the Christian faith, they are in a position of trust in their relationships with those for whom they have pastoral care.

1.3   The compassion, care and kindness of the Good Shepherd should be the hallmarks of the clergy. Unworthy behaviour disgraces the Church and undermines the gospel.

1.4   All personal and professional conduct is bounded by law and legal sanction. For the clergy, who swear the Oaths of Canonical Obedience and Allegiance, and make the Declaration of Assent, this will include ecclesiastical law as well as secular law. Thus nothing in these Guidelines should be read as suggesting that clergy stand outside the rule of criminal or civil law. Indeed, any concern about possible criminal behaviour, and in particular any information about abuse or risk of abuse will be reported by the Church authorities to the police.

Care

2   They are to sustain the community of the faithful by the ministry of word and sacrament. Priests are called to be servants and shepherds among the people to whom they are sent. They are to be messengers, watchmen and stewards of the Lord.

2.1   Caring for one another is the responsibility of the whole Church and is an extension of the justice and love of the Incarnate God disclosed in Jesus Christ. Compassion is essential to pastoral care. The clergy should enable other members of the worshipping community to share in this pastoral care, ensuring that they are recruited safely, and have the appropriate training and supervision for the tasks involved, including current training in safeguarding in accordance with the guidance issued by the House of Bishops. (See also 2.9)

Clergy should seek to ensure that churchwardens, PCCs and the wider congregation understand their responsibilities and roles in making every church a safe place for all.

2.2   In their ministry, pastoral care and working relationships, the clergy should offer equal respect and opportunity to all. They should be unbiased in their exercise of pastoral care, especially when caring for one party in a dispute between two or more people. In some cases they may need to ask another appropriate person to provide pastoral care to one of the parties.

2.3   The clergy should discern and acknowledge their own limitations of time, competence and skill. They will need to seek support, help and appropriate training and, on occasion, to refer to specialist agencies. The clergy should be aware of the help available from accredited agencies so that it can be commended where appropriate.

2.4   Clergy should always be conscious of the power dynamics involved in their pastoral care, noting both the position of trust which they hold and the power which they exercise. See also Sections 12 and 14.

2.5   The distinctions between the various roles in which the clergy exercise oversight and care are always to be recognized and acknowledged. Ministers need to be clear with those with whom they are dealing. At no time should they provide formal counselling for those in their pastoral care, even when they are accredited as counsellors in other settings. Those who wish to work as accredited counsellors should seek appropriate advice about how to maintain proper boundaries between this and their role as ordained ministers.

2.6   Similarly, where the clergy are supervising employed members of staff, or mentoring or coaching church members, there needs to be absolute clarity about the role in which they are engaging with them. The responsibility for pastoral care must not be confused with any other role.

2.7   There is risk in all pastoral work. The appropriateness of visiting and being visited alone, especially at night, needs to be assessed with care. The same assessment should also apply to other "out of hours" contact (especially through telephone calls and social media).

Consideration should be given to:
- the place of the meeting;
- the proximity of other people;
- the arrangement of furniture and lighting; and
- the dress of the minister, appropriate to the context

– which are important considerations in pastoral care. The perceptions of others need to be considered at all times, taking particular care to assess the extent to which others may experience or perceive behaviour to be inappropriate.

At times it may be appropriate to advise a third party in advance of any appointments which have been made. Keeping accurate records of appointments is helpful and good practice.

2.8   It is essential in pastoral care to acknowledge appropriate physical, sexual, emotional and psychological boundaries. Inappropriate touching or gestures of affection are to be avoided. The clergy need to be aware of what is appropriate when meeting people from different cultural traditions.

2.9   The clergy should be aware of the dangers of dependency in pastoral relationships. Manipulation, competitiveness or collusion on either side of the pastoral encounter should be avoided. Self-awareness should be part of the relationship. The responsibility for maintaining appropriate boundaries always rests with the clergy, however difficult or challenging the pastoral relationship may prove to be.

2.10   The clergy must always put first the interests of those for whom they are pastorally responsible, and act to protect them even where this requires them to override personal and professional loyalties. It is their duty to raise concerns where they believe that someone's safety or care is being compromised by the practice of colleagues, or by those in authority, or by the systems, policies or procedures with which they are expected to work. They must also encourage and support the development of a culture in which they and their colleagues can raise concerns openly and honestly. Those in authority should listen carefully to their concerns and act upon them where they are justified, enabling those who have the best interests of others at heart to raise concerns without fear of detriment to themselves.

2.11   The clergy are required to have appropriate and current training in safeguarding children and vulnerable adults. Failure to participate may result in action being taken under the Clergy Discipline Measure. The Church of England's national and diocesan policies, guidelines and requirements must be known and observed. If they become aware that someone known to have a conviction for offences against children or vulnerable adults attends their church, they must follow the guidelines for ministering to such offenders.

2.12 Clergy should be clear about the circumstances in which information about abuse of all forms, or the risk of abuse, must be reported to the statutory authorities (that is, the police or local authority children's or adult services). Children or adults who provide information about abuse need to know that their concerns will be taken seriously and that the clergy will work with them in making the referral, in order that a proper investigation can be undertaken and appropriate help be obtained.

2.13 It is essential that clergy maintain an accurate and factual written record of any safeguarding concerns or actions. They should be aware of the dangers of glossing over the conduct of fellow clergy, or even of collusion with it.

2.14 All the clergy should be aware of the circumstances in which information can and should be disclosed to third parties. To that end, they should refer to the national and diocesan safeguarding policies. When preparing for such a disclosure, the clergy should seek appropriate legal and other specialist advice, for example from the Diocesan Safeguarding Adviser. Whenever a safeguarding referral is made, clergy should always inform the Diocesan Safeguarding Adviser.

2.15 Similar requirements apply if the conduct of a colleague appears inappropriate, when advice should always be obtained and action taken.

2.16 The clergy should ensure that all communications they may have with or about children or vulnerable adults are appropriate in their tone and that they comply with relevant national and diocesan policies and guidance. This refers to the use of any means of communication, written, spoken or electronic. Anything published online is public and visible to everyone.

2.17 The clergy should take care to observe appropriate boundaries between their work and their personal life just as much in the use of social media as in "real life" encounters. They should recognize the importance of knowing themselves and their own emotional needs. Working with a spiritual director or pastoral supervisor can greatly help the development of this insight, which is difficult to achieve when working alone.

In this context it should be noted that paragraph 5.21 of *Protecting All God's Children* states: "Clergy should not expose themselves or others to material which is sexually explicit, profane, obscene, harassing, fraudulent, racially offensive, politically inflammatory, defamatory or in violation of any British, European or international law."

Reconciliation

**3   They are to teach and to admonish, to feed and provide
for his family, to search for his children in the wilderness
of this world's temptations, and to guide them through
its confusions, that they may be saved through Christ for
ever. They are to call their hearers to repentance and to
declare in Christ's name the absolution and forgiveness
of their sins.**

3.1   The ministry of reconciliation, as an extension of Jesus' own ministry,
lies at the heart of this vocation. It is to be exercised gently, patiently
and undergirded by mutual trust. It may include spiritual or godly
counsel as appropriate and as requested by those concerned; it may
include mediation between those who have found themselves at enmity
with one another.

3.2   Where it is freely sought by a penitent, a priest may exercise the formal
ministry of absolution as described in Canon B 29.

3.3   The ministry of absolution may only be exercised by the minister who
has the cure of souls of the place in question or by another priest with
that minister's permission, or by a priest who is authorized by law to
exercise ministry in that place without being subject to the control of
the minister who has the cure of souls (e.g. a priest who is licensed to
exercise ministry under the Extra-Parochial Ministry Measure 1967).
This rule is subject to an exception that permits a priest to exercise the
ministry of absolution anywhere in respect of a person who is in danger
of death or if there is "some urgent or weighty cause" (See Canon B
29.4)

3.4   Before undertaking the ministry of absolution a priest should receive
appropriate training and be familiar with any guidelines published by
the House of Bishops that relate to the exercise of this ministry.

3.5   A clear distinction must be made between pastoral conversations and
a confession that is made in the context of the ministry of absolution.
Where such a confession is to be made both the priest and the penitent
should be clear that that is the case. If a penitent makes a confession
with the intention of receiving absolution the priest is forbidden (by
the unrepealed *Proviso* to Canon 113 of the Code of 1603) to reveal or
make known to any person what has been confessed. This requirement
of absolute confidentiality applies even after the death of the penitent.

3.6 If, in the context of such a confession, the penitent discloses that he or she has committed a serious crime, such as the abuse of children or vulnerable adults, the priest must require the penitent to report his or her conduct to the police or other statutory authority. If the penitent refuses to do so the priest should withhold absolution.

3.7 The canonical duty of absolute confidentiality does not apply to anything that is said outside the context of such a confession. In particular, if information about abuse that was disclosed when seeking the ministry of absolution is repeated by the penitent outside that context the priest must follow the established procedures for reporting abuse of children or vulnerable adults.

3.8 However confidentiality extends far beyond the specific situation of the ministry of absolution. People have to be able to trust clergy with their stories, their fears, and especially their confidences. The duty of confidentiality relating to the ministry of absolution sets a standard for our ministry against which all other instances should be set and judged. Those to whom we minister must know that they can depend upon us not to disclose information which they have shared with us in confidence.

Note: *The text of this section reflects the current legal position in relation to the ministry of absolution, arising from the unrepealed proviso to Canon 113 of the Code of 1603. In September 2014 the Archbishops' Council decided to commission further theological and legal work to enable it to review, in consultation with the House of Bishops, the purpose and effect of the proviso to the Canon of 1603, with a view to enabling the General Synod to decide whether it wished to legislate to amend it.*

For further information in that connection, please see GS Misc 1085 on page 32.

Mission

4 **They are to tell the story of God's love . . . they are to unfold the Scriptures, to preach the word in season and out of season, and to declare the mighty acts of God. They are to baptize new disciples in the name of the Father, and of the Son, and of the Holy Spirit, and to walk with them in the way of Christ, nurturing them in the faith . . . they are to preside at the Lord's table and lead his people in worship, offering with them a spiritual sacrifice of praise and thanksgiving.**

4.1   Mission belongs to the whole church worldwide and is a primary calling of the clergy. Parish priests are charged with the "cure of souls", not solely the chaplaincy of congregations. As such, they have a clear responsibility, with their people, to develop appropriate practices of mission and evangelism in their parish, network or other context.

4.2   The clergy should ensure that services are thoughtfully and thoroughly prepared, matching the need and culture of the parish or institution within the Anglican tradition. Where appropriate, they should involve others in leading worship, having ensured that they are equipped to do so by providing training and preparation as necessary to support them.

4.3   The clergy should ensure that appropriate and accessible courses and discussion groups on all aspects of the Christian faith are available at regular intervals to parishioners seeking to explore, deepen or renew their faith.

4.4   Suitable preparation for Baptism, Confirmation and Marriage is a primary responsibility for the clergy.

4.5   The clergy should recognize, affirm and encourage the ministry and witness of lay people. This should include acknowledging their mission in workplaces and communities.

4.6   All schools, along with other institutions within a parish, may provide opportunities for mission and ministry, and a church school is a particular responsibility for the clergy. The clergy should seek to enhance opportunities for themselves and appropriately gifted and trained laity to contribute to the worship, religious education, pastoral care and governance in local schools and colleges.

4.7   In an increasingly "mixed economy" Church, which fosters pioneer ordained ministry and Fresh Expressions of Church as well as traditional parish ministry and mission, ministers who lead such pioneering mission are subject to the same call, responsibility and accountability.

Ministry at times of deepest need

5   **They are to bless the people in God's name. They are to resist evil, support the weak, defend the poor, and intercede for all in need. They are to minister to the sick and prepare the dying for their death.**

5.1 The clergy have a particular responsibility to minister sensitively and effectively to the sick, the dying and the bereaved. Ministry to those near to death should never be delayed.

5.2 The clergy should be familiar with and follow the current House of Bishops' *Guidelines for Good Practice in the Healing Ministry*. Existing diocesan regulations should be followed. Professional boundaries with health care professionals and chaplaincies should be observed. All reasonable steps should be taken to ensure the safety of the person receiving the healing ministry, including by ensuring that satisfactory arrangements are in place for training and accountability for those undertaking this ministry.

5.3 The clergy should be aware of and respect the boundaries between the ministry of healing and the deliverance ministry. People have a right to know what is being provided and how they will be ministered to: no one should be ministered to against their will.

5.4 Deliverance is an area of ministry where particular caution needs to be exercised, especially when ministering to someone who is in a disturbed state. The current House of Bishops' guidelines on the deliverance ministry which are known as The House of Bishops' *Guidelines for Good Practice in the Deliverance Ministry 1975* (revised 2012) should be followed and cases referred to the diocesan advisers for the deliverance ministry when necessary. The advisers' special expertise should be used in order to help as effectively as possible those who think they need this ministry.

5.5 The ministry of exorcism and deliverance may only be exercised by priests who have been specifically and personally authorized by the bishop, normally for each instance of such a ministry. If this ministry is sought in connection with a child or vulnerable adults, the Diocesan Safeguarding Adviser must be involved and may need to ensure that a referral to the statutory authorities is made, in accordance with national and diocesan safeguarding policies.

Servant Leadership

6 **Guided by the Spirit, they are to discern and foster the gifts of all God's people, that the whole Church may be built up in unity and faith.**

6.1 The clergy are called to servant ministry and leadership within the Church and the wider community.

6.2 They should develop this gift of leadership within their own ministry through prayer and training, being aware of their own natural leadership style.

6.3 The clergy should recognize and affirm lay ministry that already exists and encourage new ministries, both lay and ordained. They should be ready to assist others in discerning and fulfilling their vocation. They should actively prompt and encourage new vocations in the Church and in the world.

6.4 At times as we seek to hear God's call for the Church in this generation, the clergy will hold different views. However, all debate should be had in a spirit of respect and love, and ministers should always be willing to work with each other, whatever views are held on current topics of debate.

6.5 The clergy should promote good ecumenical relationships and encourage respect for all people of good will.

6.6 Upon resignation or retirement, the clergy should relinquish their responsibilities and should cease professional relationships with those formerly under their pastoral care. Any exception to this guideline should be formally negotiated with the bishop.

6.7 Having resigned or retired, the clergy may not minister in a former church, parish or institution unless invited by the clergy with pastoral oversight or with their express permission. Ministry in retirement is subject to the bishop granting a Licence or Permission To Officiate, and subject to the completion of safeguarding clearance and training.

Learning and Teaching

7 **Will you be diligent in prayer, in reading Holy Scripture, and in all studies that will deepen your faith and fit you to bear witness to the truth of the gospel? Will you lead Christ's people in proclaiming his glorious gospel, so that the good news of salvation may be heard in every place?**

7.1 The given daily prayer of the Church (the Daily Office) is one of the essential foundations of confident ministry centred on Christ, using the resources of the Church such as the *Book of Common Prayer*, *Common Worship*, or other authorized forms of the office.

7.2 The life of prayer, although personal, includes the praise and prayer offered in Christ's name in his church, both on earth and in heaven. Clergy should therefore seek to offer the daily prayer of the church with other members of the community in which they serve.

7.3 To pray for others in thanksgiving for the benefits of Christ is a common duty of Christians, and is a particular privilege of the ordained ministry. To intercede whether in public or in private belongs to the ways God accomplishes in his church that which he wills.

7.4 The use of conversation with a chosen companion such as a spiritual guide or with others sharing the ordained ministry is commended, recognizing the different ways in which God has called his people to relate to him, and enabled them to do so.

7.5 It is part of the mission of the clergy to teach those whom they serve both the ways and the delight of prayer, being open to learning these things as they do so.

7.6 Continued theological learning is an essential discipline for preaching and teaching, as well as for personal growth.

7.7 The clergy should set aside time for continuing ministerial education and development, including the consideration of contemporary issues and theological developments, so that their faith engages with the perceptions and concerns of this generation.

7.8 Keeping abreast of a whole variety of communicating skills is crucial to the effective and ongoing proclamation of the gospel.

7.9 Part of the clerical vocation in both preaching and teaching is a prayerful openness to being prophetic and challenging as well as encouraging and illuminating.

7.10 Great care should be taken that illustrative material from personal experience does not involve any breach of confidentiality.

Faith

8   **Do you accept the Holy Scriptures as revealing all things necessary for eternal salvation through faith in Jesus Christ? Will you faithfully minister the doctrine and sacraments of Christ as the Church of England has received them, so that the people committed to your charge may be defended against error and flourish in the faith?**

8.1   The clergy are required to make the Declaration of Assent (contained in Canon C 15) at their ordination, and at the inauguration of any new ministry within the Church of England. All should ensure that they know and understand the significance of the statements to which they have publicly given their assent, and that they can accordingly only use the forms of service authorized or allowed to be used in the Church of England.

8.2   The basis of the Church of England's understanding of doctrine and of the sacraments is set out in the Declaration of Assent, and the Preface which precedes it. The Church's clergy should uphold this understanding, having declared their commitment to it formally and publicly at the start of their ministry.

8.3   Ministers who for whatever reason find that they are unable any longer in conscience to believe, hold or teach the Christian faith as the Church of England has received it, should seek advice and help in deciding whether or not they should continue to exercise a public ministry in which they represent the Church.

Public Ministry

9   **Will you, knowing yourself to be reconciled to God in Christ, strive to be an instrument of God's peace in the Church and in the world?**

9.1   The reputation of the Church in the community depends to a great extent on the integrity and example of its clergy, who should recognize their role as public representatives of the Church. Their lives should enhance and embody the communication of the gospel.

9.2   The clergy should ensure a reasonable level of availability and accessibility to those for whom they have a pastoral care. A prompt and gracious response to all requests for help demonstrates care.

This response should be in the context of appropriate boundaries, so as not to put at risk the clergy, members of their household, or the Church.

9.3 Reconciliation lies at the heart of the gospel: "God was in Christ reconciling the world to himself" (*2 Corinthians 5.19*). The clergy should promote reconciliation in the Church and in the world wherever there are divisions, including those which exist between people of different faiths.

9.4 The call of the clergy to be servants to the community should include their prophetic ministry to those in spiritual and moral danger.

9.5 It is appropriate for the clergy to play a positive part in civic society and politics, promoting the kingdom values of justice, integrity and peace in public life, calling attention to the needs of the poor and to the godly stewardship of the world's resources.

9.6 Ministers must not be members or active supporters of any political party or other organization whose constitution, policies, objectives, activities or public statements are incompatible with the teaching of the Church of England, as defined by the House of Bishops, in relation to the equality of persons or groups of different races.

9.7 There are a number of situations where the clergy may have a conflict of interest and they should declare it, whenever that is appropriate, withdrawing from the situation if required. It is a delusion to think we can be impartial when there is a conflict of interest.

Life and Conduct

10 Will you endeavour to fashion your own life and that of your household according to the way of Christ, that you may be a pattern and example to Christ's people?

10.1 The clergy are called to an exemplary standard of moral behaviour. This goes beyond what is legally acceptable: a distinction can be made between what is legal and what is morally acceptable. There is no separation between the public and home life of the clergy: at all times and in all places they should manifest the highest standards of personal conduct.

10.2 The clergy should set an example of integrity in relationships, and faithfulness in marriage. Marital infidelity is regarded as "unbecoming or inappropriate conduct" for the purposes of the Clergy Discipline Measure. The House of Bishops' *Marriage: A Teaching Document* (1999) clearly affirms, "Sexual intercourse, as an expression of faithful intimacy, properly belongs within marriage exclusively."

10.3 Those who are called to marriage should never forget that this is also a vocation. It should not be thought to be of secondary importance to their vocation to ministry. Being a parent is likewise a holy calling and so ordained ministry should not take priority over bringing up children with Godly love, care, time and space. Similar considerations may apply to caring for other members of the family.

10.4 All should guard themselves and their family against becoming victims of harmful levels of stress. It is the calling of all Christians, whether married or not, including those with a vocation to celibacy, to take the necessary steps to nurture in holiness their lives, their friendships and their family relationships.

10.5 Good administration enables the work of ministry. Dealing promptly with correspondence and enquiries with efficiency and courtesy is essential.

10.6 The keeping of parochial registers and records to a high standard is legally required.

10.7 The clergy need to ensure that all their financial activities, whether personal or corporate, meet the highest ethical standards. There must be strict boundaries between church finance and personal moneys in order to avoid the possibility of suspicion or impropriety. This will require accurate and careful record keeping of money which is received from others, including Parochial Fees, and a proper audit trail for all money which is to be passed on to third parties including the PCC, the Diocesan Board of Finance and the tax authorities.

10.8 The clergy should never seek any personal advantage or gain by virtue of their clerical position. Those who receive personal gifts should keep a record in case of later misunderstandings or false accusations.

10.9 The clergy should take care of their physical well-being. They should not undertake any professional duties when medically advised against it, and avoid the influence of alcohol or drugs. Those who find themselves in difficulty with addictions of any kind should seek appropriate help.

10.10 Blasphemous, violent or offensive language or behaviour is unacceptable at all times. Clergy should manifest the fruit of the Spirit: see Galatians 5.22-23.

Discipline

11 **Will you work with your fellow servants in the gospel for the sake of the kingdom of God? Will you accept and minister the discipline of this Church, and respect authority duly exercised within it?**

11.1 The clergy should know how ecclesiastical law shapes their exercise of office and ministry, and should respect such regulations as are put in place by the Church. They should familiarize themselves with *The Canons of the Church of England*, and with any regulations made by the bishop of the diocese in which they serve.

11.2 The authority of churchwardens and lay people elected or appointed to office in the local church is to be respected and affirmed.

11.3 The clergy serve under the authority of the bishop both in the ministry to which they have been appointed, and in the diocese as a whole. At their ordination and at every new appointment they take an Oath of Canonical Obedience, committing themselves to live within the framework provided by scriptures, creeds, historic formularies, canons and legislation which govern their ministry within the Church of England.

11.4 They should participate actively in the life and work of chapter, deanery, archdeaconry, and diocese, giving support and respect to ordained and lay colleagues and to those who exercise the responsibility of oversight and leadership.

11.5 Any member of the clergy who is arrested for an offence, however minor, and whether or not charges are brought, is required by the Clergy Discipline Measure to report this fact within 28 days to their bishop. However, clergy who are questioned by the police in relation to a possible arrest should also report that fact.

11.6 Any ordained person who is the subject of an allegation of misconduct in relation to a child or vulnerable adult or of domestic abuse, whether in their public ministry or in their home life, must report this fact straight away to their bishop.

11.7 Clergy whose marriages break down and who are divorced, or have an order of judicial separation made against them, on grounds of their adultery, unreasonable behaviour or desertion by them of their spouse can have a penalty under the Clergy Discipline Measure imposed on them as a result. Any member of the clergy who is a party to a divorce petition or an application for an order for judicial separation should therefore obtain legal advice in respect of their position under the Clergy Discipline Measure before any steps are taken in the matrimonial proceedings.

11.8 Clergy are under a duty to inform their bishop when they are divorced, or have an order of judicial separation made against them.

11.9 The highest standards are expected of the clergy in respect of their personal relationships, not least in respect of their relationships with those in their pastoral care. In particular, the clergy must never have sexual or inappropriate relationships with those aged 16 or 17, or vulnerable adults. A breach of this requirement, in addition to being treated as a disciplinary matter, will be referred to the local authority designated officer. In some cases it may constitute a criminal offence. Anyone found guilty of a criminal or disciplinary offence of this kind is likely to be removed from office and referred to the Disclosure and Barring Service which has power to bar them from work with children and/or vulnerable adults.

11.10 Discretion should be used in all forms of communication including when sending messages by email or text, or when visiting social networking sites or blogs, or holding conversations using cameras or microphones via the internet, much of which relies upon insecure forms of data transmission.

It is advisable for clergy to maintain a distinct email address for their ministry which is not shared with others in the household, and email correspondence received should be accessible only to the person to whom it is sent.

Confidentiality in all forms of correspondence must be respected and maintained whether written or electronic.

11.11 The clergy must remember that they are public figures whose opinions when proffered have weight and significance. In using social media ministers should always assume that anything they post or contribute is in the public domain and will be shared. The power of the internet for doing harm as well as good must always be borne carefully in mind and weighed before saying anything which may prove be damaging to oneself as well as to others.

11.12 Close attention must be given to secure all forms of data, including traditional paper records. In particular, data held on mobile or desktop computing equipment and on mobile devices should have secure passwords and up-to-date security software.

Trust

12 **In the name of our Lord we bid you remember the greatness of the trust that is now to be committed to your charge. Remember always with thanksgiving that the treasure now to be entrusted to you is Christ's own flock, bought by the shedding of his blood on the cross. It is to him that you will render account for your stewardship of his people.**

12.1 The development of trust is of primary importance for honest relationships within ministry.

12.2 The clergy are placed in a position of power and authority over others, in pastoral relationships, with lay colleagues, and sometimes with other ministers. In all forms of ministry, in leadership, teaching, preaching and presiding at worship, the clergy should resist all temptation to exercise power inappropriately. This power needs to be used to sustain others and harness their strengths, and not to abuse, bully, manipulate or denigrate.

12.3 Pastoral care should never seek to remove the autonomy given to the individual. In pastoral situations the other party should be allowed the freedom to make decisions that may be mistaken unless children or vulnerable adults are thereby placed at risk in which case the advice of the Diocesan Safeguarding Adviser must be sought.

12.4 The clergy should thankfully acknowledge their own God-given sexuality. They should not seek sexual advantage, emotionally or physically, in the exercise of their ministry.

12.5 A person seeking pastoral guidance and counsel has the right to expect that the minister concerned will not pass on to a third party confidential information so obtained, without their consent or other lawful authority. Exceptions to the general position include information concerning the commission of a crime or other misconduct, where there is a requirement that the information be disclosed. If a minister has grounds for considering that that exception may apply, or that the disclosure reveals a risk to children or vulnerable adults, he or she should consult the diocesan registrar and, in cases involving safeguarding issues, the Diocesan Safeguarding Adviser.

12.6 Unless otherwise agreed, the clergy are accordingly not at liberty to share confidential information with their spouses, family or friends.

12.7   The content and process of a pastoral relationship may need to be shared with certain other people, such as a supervisor or supervisory group, consultant or other involved colleagues. Such sharing needs to be carefully restricted so that it does not involve any breach of confidence.

12.8   It is important to safeguard the right of parishioners to share personal information with one minister and not another. In a team situation, it may be advisable to create a policy to avoid the danger to ministers within a team of being manipulated and divided by the sharing of personal information with one and not another.

12.9   Ministers who handle personal information about individuals are under the same legal obligations to protect that information under the Data Protection Act 1998 as anyone else. When help or advice is being sought, any note-taking should be mutually agreed wherever possible. If notes contain any information about a living individual which is capable of identifying that individual ("personal data") the notes will be subject to the Act. Information about the Act may be found at www.ico.gov.uk

12.10 The minister of a parish is required by law to provide for the publication of the banns of marriage and the solemnization of holy matrimony for those within their cure, subject to any impediments which may exist in law to their union. Canon B 33 requires the minister to make inquiries as to the existence of any reasons which may prevent the marriage from taking place, and should seek appropriate advice from the diocesan registrar or the civil authorities in any case of doubt. The clergy should also be aware of the House of Bishops' Guidance on the Marriage of Non-EEA (European Economic Area) Nationals, and the requirement to follow that guidance.

12.11 There is much helpful advice in the Faculty Office publication, *Anglican Marriage in England and Wales: A Guide to the Law for the Clergy*. Copies can be purchased from the Faculty Office at 1 The Sanctuary, Westminster, SW1P 3JT.

12.12 It is the duty of every parochial minister to officiate at the funerals or interment of those who die within their cure, or any parishioners or persons whose names are entered on the church electoral roll of their parish whether deceased within their cure or elsewhere. (Canon B 38). This obligation includes not only funeral services which take place at the parish church, but those which are held in a crematorium or cemetery. Others will also be involved in the care of the bereaved, including funeral directors and cemetery and crematorium staff.

The clergy should maintain good professional relationships with all such to ensure appropriate care for the relatives of those who have died.

12.13 Ministers must not officiate or otherwise exercise ministry outside the area of the benefice to which they have been instituted or licensed without the consent of the minister with the cure of souls. This is subject to a statutory entitlement of the minister of a parish to perform a funeral service in any crematorium or cemetery that is situated in another parish without consent provided that the deceased died or was resident in the minister's own parish or was on the electoral roll of that parish at the time of his or her death.

12.14 When officiating at weddings and funerals the clergy should ensure that only those fees prescribed by the Archbishops' Council in a Parochial Fees Order, reasonable travel expenses and genuine extras are requested from those with whom they make arrangements. When a marriage service or funeral service is being conducted only statutory fees and genuine extras (such as payments to organists, singers and bellringers) may be charged.

Well-being

13   **You cannot bear the weight of this calling in your own strength, but only by the grace and power of God. Pray therefore that your heart may daily be enlarged and your understanding of the Scriptures enlightened. Pray earnestly for the gift of the Holy Spirit.**

13.1 The clergy minister by grace through their own broken humanity, being aware of their own need to receive ministry.

13.2 In exercising their ministry, the clergy respond to the call of our Lord Jesus Christ. The development of their discipleship is in the discipline of prayer, worship, Bible study and the discernment of the prompting of the Holy Spirit. The clergy should make sure that time and resources are available for their own personal and spiritual life and take responsibility for their own ongoing training and development.

13.3 Spiritual discernment can be facilitated by sharing the journey of faith with another person. A minister should have someone outside the work situation to whom to turn for help.

13.4 Ministers holding office under common tenure have a legal obligation to cooperate in arrangements made by the diocesan bishop for ministerial development review, and to participate in appropriate continuing ministerial education. Ministers who are not subject to common tenure should also, as a matter of good practice, ensure that arrangements are in place for their ministry to be reviewed on a regular basis and for their ongoing ministerial education.

13.5 Both formal ministerial development review and discussion with a spiritual director or companion should offer the opportunity for the clergy to reflect on whether they are giving sufficient time and attention to family life, friendship, recreation and renewal and to consider any health issues.

Care for the Carers

14 **Brothers and sisters, you have heard how great is the charge that these ordinands are ready to undertake . . . Will you continually pray for them? Will you uphold and encourage them in their ministry?**

14.1 "Care for the carers" is fundamental. The clergy need to be supported and the laity have a particular and significant role in the pastoral care of the clergy.

The clergy and those who support them should be aware of the Ministry Division publication *Dignity at Work* (2008) and its recommendations concerning bullying, harassment, and accusation at work.

14.2 The bishop takes responsibility for the welfare of the clergy when receiving the oath of canonical obedience. This responsibility is shared with suffragan and area bishops, archdeacons, and rural and area deans.

14.3 Care of the clergy is a responsibility shared between the PCC and Diocesan Authorities.

Many of these responsibilities are spelled out in the *Statement of Particulars* under Common Tenure and in Diocesan Regulations. The PCC is responsible for the provision of adequate administrative assistance, reimbursement in full of ministerial expenses (see The Parochial Expenses of the Clergy, Ministry Division, 2002) available online at *www.churchofengland.org/clergy-office-holders/remuneration-and-conditions-of-service-committee/the-parochial-expenses-of-the-clergy.aspx*) and for ensuring a safe environment in the church and its surroundings in which to work.

Where the PCC is the relevant housing provider, it has responsibilities for the maintenance and upkeep of the clergy housing. The responsibilities of Bishop and Diocese are as set out in the *Statement of Particulars* and Diocesan Clergy Handbook, and in the *Green Guide* published by the Church Commissioners. The *Statement of Particulars* includes provision for holidays, an annual retreat, upkeep of the parsonage house, and entitlement to release for extra-parochial ministry.

14.4 As part of good stewardship, those who occupy either a parsonage house or housing provided by the Diocese or PCC must take proper care of the property and should be aware of the requirement to allow access for both inspections and works to take place.

14.5 Power is exercised and experienced in many ways, and the clergy should beware of the potential of using their position to bully others. Equally those who have the responsibility of caring for the clergy should be aware that bullying can be exercised both by church authorities and by parishioners.

14.6 The clergy should be encouraged to develop opportunities for mutual support and pastoral care within chapters, cell groups, or other peer-groupings. All the clergy should also be encouraged to have a spiritual director, soul friend or confessor to support their spiritual life and help to develop their growth in self-understanding. If required, help should be given in finding such a person.

14.7 In ministries where the clergy have both a sector and a parochial responsibility, there should be a clear understanding between diocese, parish and the minister concerned about where the boundaries lie.

14.8 Support and advice on the practical, psychological and emotional issues involved should be readily available to clergy approaching retirement and to their families.

14.9 The bishop and those exercising pastoral care of the clergy should both by word and example actively encourage the clergy to adopt a healthy life-style which should include adequate time for leisure, through taking days off and their full holidays, developing interests outside their main area of ministry, and maintaining a commitment to the care and development of themselves and their personal relationships. Helping the clergy understand and overcome unrealistic expectations needs to be a priority.

Grant, Lord, that we may live in your fear,
die in your favour, rest in your peace,
rise in your power and reign in your glory;
for your own beloved Son's sake,
Jesus Christ our Lord.

William Laud (1573–1645)

Remember, O Lord, what thou hast wrought in us
and not what we deserve;
and as thou hast called us to thy service,
make us worthy of our calling;
through Jesus Christ our Lord.

The Prayer Book as proposed in 1928

Postscript

These guidelines are not meant to be a burden, nor do they pretend to be complete. They should help the clergy discover and experience how great is the freedom to which they are called and the joy that the gift of an ordained life brings. We are to remember the injunction of St Paul to be "happy in the Lord at all times" and to rejoice always in his abiding presence.

We recognize, too, that we are not alone, that we cannot do all these things by ourselves in our own strength, but only by the grace of God and through the power of his Spirit working in and through us; for as the Prayer Book Ordinal puts it, in the Declaration to those being ordained to the office of priest, we are called to "apply ourselves wholly to this one thing and to draw all our cares and studies this way" and that we will "continually pray to God the Father, by the mediation of our only Saviour Jesus Christ, for the assistance of the Holy Ghost".

So we pray that our lives may be sanctified to this end, for the sake of those whom we seek to serve. For the ordained life of a bishop, a priest or a deacon, for whom these guidelines are designed, is indeed of "what dignity and of how great importance", but also of "so great excellency and so great difficulty" that we all need help and encouragement along the way – and it is in that spirit that the Guidelines are offered.

So it is our prayer that, by our lives and in our work, through all we do and by what we are called to be, we may honour God's holy name and be faithful to the vocation he has given us, that his salvation may be proclaimed in all the world. May we be found worthy of our calling!

Prebendary David Houlding
Pro-Prolocutor of the Convocation of Canterbury
Chair of the Working Party

A theological reflection

The Very Revd Dr Francis Bridger

Dean of Brechin, Scottish Episcopal Church and Ecclesiastical Professor of Anglican Studies, Fuller Theological Seminary, Pasadena, California

In the decade since the Church of England adopted the original version of these Guidelines, events have reinforced the importance of ensuring good practice in professional conduct of the clergy. It is timely, therefore, that the philosophy and theology that undergird the Guidelines set out below are articulated once more. For although it may still seem to some clergy that the existence of a set of guidelines implies a lack of trust in their integrity and an intrusion into sacred vocation, the reality is that the Church must continually strive to retain the confidence of a society that has observed scandals within the Church that have undermined such confidence. The Church can no longer count on an unquestioning presumption of trustworthiness and it would be wrong to do so.

The purpose of this reflection therefore is twofold: firstly to rehearse the pragmatic reasons why professional guidelines exist; and secondly to set out a number of theological principles which inform them.

Pragmatic Considerations

The pragmatics are straightforward: from the perspective of its internal life, the Church now has in place a clear procedure for clergy discipline in the shape of the Clergy Discipline Measure that has been in effect from 2006. Since discipline requires an understanding of what does and does not count as acceptable professional behaviour, it follows that guidelines for practice are apposite. It is worth noting, also, that over the last 10 years, Anglican provinces and dioceses around the world have adopted their own versions of professional guidelines.

From a broader perspective, there is a continuing need for the Church to respond to historic and current social pressures for greater regulation of *all* professions. To date, this has been achieved mainly by means of *self*-regulation, and therefore it is reasonable to expect that the Church reaffirm its willingness to engage in the same kind of self-examination as have others. The simple truth is that a great deal more public concern now exists about the integrity of previously-respected professions: no longer are people willing to give professionals the benefit of the doubt merely because they are professionals.[1] They are properly subject to scrutiny and criticism in a way that was not true a generation ago. This constitutes a sizeable challenge to the Church, for it is no longer – if it ever was – credible that it should expect to remain immune from such scrutiny. The need for accountability and transparency is as strong now as it was when the Guidelines were first published.[2]

Clergy Discipline procedures and the Professional Guidelines are designed to protect three parties: the accused, the accuser and the Church. It is important to mention the last of these because it can easily be forgotten that professional ethics are not simply a matter for individuals. While they undoubtedly exist to guide and protect individuals they also serve to safeguard the profession. They are an expression of mutual accountability and responsibility. When one clergyman or woman acts unprofessionally, he or she threatens to bring the Church as a whole into disrepute – witness the ripple effect of scandals. As Eric Mount has commented: "Moral responsibility includes being responsible people within institutions."[3] Or in St Paul's words, "We are members one of another" (*Ephesians 4.25*).[4]

It is important to appreciate, moreover, that whereas the Clergy Discipline Measure provides a mechanism whereby justice can be done and be seen to be done (not least for the accused), the Guidelines set out here supply a framework for behaviour that reflects the highest standards to which all clergy, by virtue of their calling as well as their office, should aspire.

Pragmatic reasons in themselves, though, are not enough. They are a necessary – but not sufficient – justification for self-regulation by the Church if it is to be prepared for the sort of scrutiny presupposed by contemporary society. It is here that a *theology of professional responsibility* becomes central. And it is to this we now turn.

---

1.   On the debate as to how far the clergy should be understood as professionals and therefore to what extent the models employed by "the professions" are relevant, see Karen Lebacqz and Joseph D. Driskill, *Ethics and Spiritual Care*, Nashville: Abingdon Press 2000, chap. 2. Also Eric Mount Jr, *Professional Ethics in Context*, Louisville: Westminster/John Knox Press 1990, chaps 2 and 3.

2   See the *Interim and Final Reports of the Commissaries Appointed by the Archbishop of Canterbury in Relation to a Visitation upon the Diocese of Chichester* (2012 and 2013) available at http://rowan-williams.archbishopofcanterbury.org/articles.php/2604/archbishops-chichester-visitation-interim-report-published and at http://www.archbishopofcanterbury.org/articles.php/5055/archbishops-chichester-visitation-final-report-published

3   Eric Mount Jr, *Professional Ethics in Context: Institutions, Images and Empathy*, Louisville: Westminster/John Knox Press 1990, p.45.

4   Significantly, Paul uses the language of mutual interdependence as justification for the code of community ethics he goes on to outline in this passage (vv.26f).

Professional Responsibility

The starting point for any discussion of professionalism must be the principle of *vocation*. It is axiomatic that ordained ministry is first and foremost a calling that originates with the purposes of God, is intuited by the individual and is then discerned by the Church. The sense that they are engaged in a vocation rather than a career is fundamental to clergy identity and self-understanding.[5] Unfortunately, however, this is sometimes used as a kind of knock-down argument against the introduction of a professional code of practice on the grounds that "to 'professionalise' pastoral ministry is to accept uncritically a culture of managerialism that reduces ministry to a set of competencies and tasks and ignores its spiritual, transcendent dimension".[6]

While there is something to be said for a critique of the competency culture that the Church has sometimes seemed to adopt without question (the so-called "management by tick-box" approach that can often be found in clergy review processes, for example), it needs to be remembered that: (a) historically, the notion of "profession" has its roots in a religious connection between profession and vocation;[7] (b) the idea of *professio* (from which the term profession derives) carries with it the meaning of "standing for something" or "value laden"; (c) the identification of professionalism with technocratic expertise is a modern development which has served unduly and untheologically to narrow the concept; and (d) by means of a theology of vocation, it becomes possible to reinvest the idea of profession with a transcendent, moral dimension, thereby drawing the sting of critics in one respect at least. In Richard Gula's words, "Aligning 'having a vocation' with 'being a professional'... affirms all that we do in ministry is a response to the presence of God in and through the community calling us to act on its behalf as signs and agents of God's love."[8]

In the light of this, the criticism that guidelines amount to an unwarranted concession to managerialism must be seen as misplaced. They simply set out what it means to act in a manner consistent with a calling to ministry and should be seen as an attempt to work out in concrete terms the practice of vocation in a

---

5   For a recent discussion see Nigel Peyton and Caroline Gatrell, *Managing Clergy Lives: Obedience, Sacrifice, Intimacy*, London: Bloomsbury 2013, chap. 4.

6   Richard M. Gula, *Ethics in Pastoral Ministry*, NY: Paulist Press 1996, p.11.

7   Thus Darrell Reeck notes that, "Judaeo-Christian culture from Biblical times through the Reformation imbued the concept of *profession* with the moral concept of service grounded in a religious vision of God working together with people for the improvement of all creation. The doctrine of the vocation or calling became the religious and moral theme that most illuminated the meaning of the professions and professional work." Darrell Reeck, *Ethics for the Professions: A Christian Perspective*, Minneapolis: Augsburg 1982, p.33 quoted in Joe E. Trull & James E. Carter, *Ministerial Ethics*, Broadman & Holman, 1993, p.25.

8   Gula, as above, p.14.

contemporary setting. As a result, "profession", in a clergy context, must be seen as possessing not one meaning but two: on one hand to describe the sociological reality of a group of people who operate according to conventions and practices developed by the group; and on the other, as an indication that this group stands for – professes – a set of transcendent values and principles which derive from a theology of vocation. Both senses of the term profession must be kept in mind.

From the principle of vocation follows the question: a vocation to what? The most obvious answer is "to serve". But to serve whom? Theologically, service is firstly towards God and only secondly towards human beings. Moreover, such service is only possible through relationship. This, in turn, requires the teasing out of a cluster of concepts that shape the notions of relationship and relationality, and at the centre of this cluster lies the idea of covenant.

1. Covenant

The concept of covenant represents the wellspring from which a theology of professional responsibility flows. Its significance can be demonstrated by contrasting it with the concept that governs secular models of professional relationship, namely that of *contract*. As Richard Gula has pointed out, the two are close cousins but there are crucial differences. Contracts define the specific nature of the relationship and the precise rights and duties that follow from it. Neither party can expect the other to go beyond the specified contractual duties, and each has the liberty to refuse requests to do so. Indeed, the expectation is that such requests will not be made or granted except *in extremis*. "The contract model acknowledges human limitations of the contracting parties since it clearly distinguishes rights and duties. It circumscribes the kind and amount of service being sought and offered."[9] By contrast, the biblical model of covenant – exemplified most powerfully by the covenant relationship between God and his people – is based upon grace. The covenant partners are bound together not by a set of legal requirements but by the relational nexus of gracious initiative followed by thankful response. Covenant goes further than the carefully defined obligations contained within a contract to the need for further actions that might be required by love. "When we act according to a covenant, we look beyond the minimum... Partners in a covenant are willing to go the extra mile to make things work out."[10]

---

9   Gula p.15.

10   Gula p.15.

It is this graciousness – the readiness "to make room for the gratuitous, not just the gratuities"[11] – that distinguishes covenant from contract and gives ministry its distinctive quality. Rooted in the covenant love of God, the covenantal ministry of clergy mirrors that of Christ himself who gave himself freely for the sake of the world and "who, though he was in the form of God, did not count equality with God a thing to be grasped but emptied himself, taking the form of a servant" (*Philippians 2.6-7*). The covenant model is, in the end, profoundly Christological.

The implication of this is that those who are called to ordained ministry must act out of a covenantal rather than a contractual motivation and mindset. They must be "willing to go the extra mile" which means that they must be prepared to allow their ministry to be shaped by the needs of others rather than their own preconceptions of autonomy. But how might this be worked out? This leads us to two further principles: agape and virtue.

2. Agape

In a discussion of agape and pastoral care, Simon Robinson notes that agape and covenant are intimately connected in a number of ways. In the first place, both are based upon gift, for just as covenant is gracious, so agape is a matter of gift-love. In pastoral terms, agape "is not based upon any contractual terms" but is "a way of knowing the other, the ground of care for the other".[12] Pastoral relationships are thus governed by agape. Secondly, agape involves faithfulness and constancy. The minister remains true to the other person whatever he or she has done since "agape promises to be there whatever the response from the other".[13] Thirdly, agape allows for a measure of relational open-endedness rather than placing rigid limitations on the growth of a pastoral relationship. This is not to deny the importance of boundaries; yet, at the same time, it "nourishes rather than limits relationships" and "is always searching for the good of the other ... is always open to the possibilities of the other".[14] From this it can be seen that agapeic love is not conditioned by the attraction or achievement of the other but "loves the other simply because they are the other". It is "a love which does not base itself on the action of the other, a disinterested love which is not based in a partial way on the other".[15]

---

11   Gula p.15.

12   Simon J. Robinson, *Agape, Moral Meaning and Pastoral Counselling*, Cardiff: Aureus Publishing 2001, pp.44,43. For a recent discussion of agape as the basis for a comprehensive Christian ethic, see Stanley J. Grenz, *The Moral Quest: Foundations of Christian Ethics*, Leicester: Apollos 1997, chap 8.

13   Robinson p.45.

14   Robinson p.45.

15   Robinson p.44.

How, in turn, should this theology be applied? Secular pastoral counselling has developed five operational principles as the basis for its professional codes. If we invest them with the theological concept of agape, it becomes possible to construe them as a principled framework for ethical practice in ordained ministry:

i.   the promotion of autonomy for the counsellee (understood as the ability to make self-chosen decisions)

ii.   the duty of the counsellor to act for the positive good of the counsellee (the principle of beneficence);

iii. the responsibility of the counsellor to do no harm (the principle of non-maleficence);

iv.   the obligation to act justly in the counsellee's best interests (the principle of justice);

v.   the counsellor's commitment to trustworthiness (the principle of fidelity).

While the term agape does not explicitly appear, from a theological perspective it can be discerned as the theological meta-principle lying behind all five. And if we were to substitute the terms "parishioner" for "counsellee" and "minister" for "counsellor", the transference to a set of principles for Christian ministry becomes clear.

What is equally clear, too, is that while one purpose of this framework is to protect the counsellor/minister, its fundamental emphasis is on the needs of the client/parishioner. In Robinson's language, the principles are directed towards the well-being of the Other. The rights of the helper are secondary to the good of the one who seeks help. This in turn means that those of us who are called upon to offer ministerial care must be prepared to allow our independence to be qualified as we test our ministry against the demands of professional guidelines informed by agape. The Guidelines give substance to this.

Nowhere is the importance of agapeic principles more clearly seen than in the issue of power. Within the relationship between clergy and parishioners, it is crucial to appreciate that power is used asymmetrically. That is to say, the clergyman or woman is more powerful than the person seeking help. Although self-evident upon reflection, this is a fact which is all too easily overlooked. At its worst, the wielding of asymmetrical power leads to abuse, sexual and otherwise. The vicar who uses her power to coerce, manipulate or bully an individual into agreement is every bit as abusive – albeit in a different way – as the vicar who uses his status to satisfy his sexual desires. Both are exercising power to achieve their own ends in contravention of the principles above.

In reflecting on this, we are helped by the work of Rollo May who has developed a typology of power that enables us to identify what kind of power is being used at any given time.[16] According to May, power can be discerned under five headings:

i.   *exploitative* power which dominates by force and coercion;
ii. *manipulative* power which controls by more subtle and covert psychological means;
iii. *competitive* power which is ambiguous since it can be used constructively where parties are relatively equal but is destructive where they are unequal (as in most pastoral relationships);
iv. *nutritive* power which sustains and empowers;
v.   *integrative* power which takes the freedom of others seriously and seeks to harness the other person's (potential) strengths.

This typology offers a grid by which particular ministerial exercises of power can be assessed. The first two types clearly fall outside a covenantal/agapeic understanding of ministry since they are not concerned with the needs or good of the other person at all. The third is questionable, though capable of constructive use in some situations. The fourth and fifth accord well with a theology of covenant and agape because they arise out of a desire to further the best interests of the other.

From a ministerial perspective, therefore, "the moral challenge is to see that in our interaction with others, the right use of power moves away from dominating others through exploitation and manipulation, and that it moves toward liberating others through nutrient and integrative acts of power".[17] When seeking to achieve our objectives – whether with a group of people or in a one-to-one relationship – we must ask ourselves what kind of power we are seeking to exercise and for whose benefit? If the answer to either of these questions is ourselves, we need to return to the five agapeic principles and reflect again.

In summary, therefore, it can be seen that if ministry is to be based on a concept of covenantal responsibility from which agapeic practice flows, this will require a more substantive set of professional criteria than a simple appeal to the beatitudes or any other general idea. As the example of how power might be exercised shows, a more complex approach is needed if we are to grasp both the theological nature of ministerial relationships and the implications for practice that must follow.

---

16   Rollo May, *Power and Innocence*, New York: W.W. Norton & Co. 1972, chap. 5. See also Karen Lebacqz, *Professional Ethics: Power and Paradox*, Nashville: Abingdon Press 1985.

17   Richard Gula, as above, p.86.

3.   Virtue

Ethical behaviour, though, is not just a matter of adherence to rules or principles. The revival of virtue ethics among moral philosophers and theologians in recent years reminds us that the *character* of the professional is as important as the *moral* code to which he or she adheres.[18] The ethics of conduct must be shaped by the ethics of character and the ethics of integrity.

What does this mean? According to William Willimon, character can be defined as the "basic moral orientation that gives unity, definition and direction to our lives by forming our habits into meaningful and predictable patterns that have been determined by our dominant convictions".[19] What we do is governed by who we are. As Stanley Hauerwas notes, each of us makes moral choices arising out of "the dispositions, experience, traditions, heritage and virtues that he or she has cultivated".[20]

From this, two points stand out: firstly, the Christian minister must *deliberately* cultivate Christian character and virtues and not leave them to chance. In Pauline language, he or she must seek the fruits of the Spirit: love, joy, peace, patience, kindness, goodness, faithfulness, gentleness, self-control (*Galatians 5.22-23*). When we ask what this might entail in terms of professional ethics, Karen Lebacqz argues for two central virtues: trustworthiness and prudence. The former is a matter of integrity or honour so that the minister is recognized as a "trustworthy trustee". The latter has to do with wise judgement or discernment. The combination of both is necessary for the minister to develop an instinct for doing the right.

Secondly, we are brought back to the idea of "habits of the heart" suggested (inter alia) by Willimon. Because these arise out of the kind of people we are, our theological convictions and spiritual practices are crucial to professional life. We are formed by the beliefs we hold, the ways in which we relate to God and the communities to which we belong. Doctrine, ethics and spirituality go hand in hand "to the point of behaving ethically most of the time as though by instinct".[21] The Guidelines' use of the Ordinal as their organizing framework recognizes this and reminds us that the sustenance of virtue cannot be a matter of indifference or fortuitousness. The *deliberate* cultivation of spiritual life is crucial.

---

18   On the importance of virtue ethics, see Joseph J. Kotva, The Christian Case for Virtue Ethics, Washington DC: Georgetown University Press 1996.

19   quoted in Trull and Carter, as above, p.47.

20   Trull and Carter p.47.

21   Walter E. Wiest & Elwyn A. Smith, Ethics in Ministry: A Guide for the Professional, Minneapolis: Fortress Press 1990, p.182.

Having said this, it has to be remembered that behind all Christian versions of virtue ethics stands the truth and reality of divine grace. The power to be and do right flows from the free self-giving of God in Christ. And it is through the indwelling Holy Spirit that we are enabled to grow in character and virtue. We become trustworthy trustees and are sustained in ministry by the activity of God in us. Ministerial guidelines may set the boundaries but only by grace can we live them out. In Richard Gula's words, "If we are to minister in the spirit of Jesus and continue in our own time his mission of proclaiming the reign of God, then we must be free enough in ourselves to accept God's offer of love and so be free for others to enable them to let go of whatever keeps them from accepting divine love as well".[22]

Conclusion

This has necessarily been a brief survey of the issues and principles that underlie the Guidelines: a mapping of the terrain rather than an exhaustive journey through it. We have seen how the Church can no longer stand back from addressing the issue of what it means to act professionally in today's social climate. We have noted that to develop a culture of professional ethics will require not just a set of criteria that govern good practice but also virtuous character based on theology and spirituality. Above all, we are reminded that the foundational value for all Christian ethics is the uniquely Christian gift of agape. Without this we are but clanging cymbals, professional or otherwise.

Francis Bridger
Brechin
Trinity 2014

---

22   Gula, as above, p.29.

GS Misc 1085

The Ministry of Absolution

General Synod

1. At its meeting on 30 September the Archbishops' Council considered what advice to offer to the Convocations on its treatment, in the proposed revision of the *Guidelines for the Professional Conduct of the Clergy*, of the ministry of absolution for which provision is made in Canon B 29. The Annex to this paper sets out the background to the revision process.

2. The Working Party preparing the revised draft of the revised Guidelines on behalf of the Convocations proposed that the section dealing with "Reconciliation" should, amongst other matters, describe the current legal position in relation to the formal ministry of absolution.

3. The legal position in that respect is governed by the unrepealed proviso to Canon 113 of the Code of 1603, which reads as follows:

    "Provided always, that if any man confess his secret and hidden sins to the minister, for the unburdening of his conscience, and to receive spiritual consolation and ease of mind from him; we do not in any way bind the said minister by this our Constitution, but do straitly charge and admonish him, that he do not at any time reveal and make known to any person whatsoever any crime or offence so committed to his trust and secrecy (except they be such crimes as by the laws of this realm his own life may be called into question for concealing the same), under pain of irregularity."

4. This is the one provision of the 1603 Code which was not repealed as part of the complete overhaul of the Canons of the Church of England in the 1950s, which led to the present Code being enacted by the Convocations in 1964 and 1969.

5. The effect of the proviso is that, where the formal ministry of absolution as described in Canon B 29 is sought, if the penitent makes a confession with the intention of receiving absolution, the priest is forbidden to reveal or make known to any person what has been

confessed. That requirement of absolute confidentiality applies even after the death of the penitent.[1]

6.   The Archbishops' Council recognized that the practice of the ministry of absolution has a well-established place in the life of the Church of England, playing an important part in the spiritual life of some of its members and representing a significant aspect of the ministry of some of its clergy.

7.   However, the Council also recognized the responsibility of the Church to protect children and vulnerable adults from harm, and the force of the argument that the legal framework of the Church should accordingly, in all respects, be such as to enable those who present a risk to children and vulnerable adults to be identified – both so that they can be held to account for past wrongs and be prevented from doing further harm. The Council is also aware that there has been some wider debate as to whether Parliament should legislate to make it an offence not to report evidence of child abuse to the statutory agencies.

8.   The Council therefore decided to commission further theological and legal work to enable it to review, in consultation with the House of Bishops, the purpose and effect of the unrepealed proviso to the Canon of 1603, with a view to enabling the Synod to decide whether it wished to legislate to amend it. At their November meeting the Council will consider the terms of that review and who should conduct it, with a view to putting their proposals in those respects to the House of Bishops when it meets in December.

9.   In the light of its decision, the Council invited the Working Party undertaking the revision of the Guidelines to consider further the section on "Reconciliation". It has now been amended to make clear that the present law, which is explained there, is now to be the subject of a review.

William Fittall
SECRETARY GENERAL
22 October 2014

---

1   As is apparent from the text, the Canon allowed for an exception to the duty of confidentiality where non-disclosure could have rendered the priest himself vulnerable to prosecution for a capital offence. This provision was, however, never operative since by 1603 Parliament had already legislated to abolish the common law capital offence for a person who had knowledge of a treasonous plot not to reveal the plot to the Crown. Instead, it had created a statutory offence of misprision of treason, with a maximum sentence of life imprisonment.

Documents referred to in the text

Preface
Common Worship Ordination Services 2007 (Known as *The Ordinal*)
Clergy Discipline Measure 2003
Ecclesiastical Offices (Terms of Service) Measure 2009

Safeguarding
2.17   *Protecting All God's Children* The Child Protection Policy of the Church of England 4th edition, 2010 (House of Bishops)

Reconciliation
3.2   The Canons of the Church of England
Note: GS Misc 1085 is included in this document at page 32

Ministry at times of deepest need
5.2   *Guidelines for Good Practice in the Healing Ministry* – House of Bishops
5.4   *Guidelines for Good Practice in the Deliverance Ministry 1975 (revised 2012)* – House of Bishops

Trust
12.9   The Data Protection Act 1998
12.11   *Anglican Marriage in England and Wales: A Guide to the Law for the Clergy* (published by the Faculty Office, 1 The Sanctuary, Westminster, SW1P 3JT)

Care for the Carers
14.1   *Dignity at Work* (2008) – Ministry Division publication
14.3   *The Parochial Expenses of the Clergy* (2002) – Ministry Division publication
Clergy Terms and Conditions of Service (Common Tenure)
Parsonages: A Design Guide (The Green Guide) – Church Commissioners publication

Safeguarding and relevant documents

Child Protection

The Church of England, in all aspects of its life, is committed to and will champion the protection of children and young people both in society as a whole and in its own community.

It fully accepts, endorses and will implement the principle enshrined in the Children Act 1989, that the welfare of the child is paramount. The Church of England will foster and encourage best practice within its community by setting standards for working with children and young people and by supporting parents in the care of their children.

It will work with statutory bodies, voluntary agencies and other faith communities to promote the safety and well-being of children and young people. It is committed to acting promptly whenever a concern is raised about a child or young person or about the behaviour of an adult, and will work with the appropriate statutory bodies when an investigation into child abuse is necessary.

The Church of England is committed to encouraging an environment where all people and especially those who may be vulnerable for any reason are able to worship and pursue their faith journey with encouragement and in safety. Everyone, whether they see themselves as vulnerable or not, will receive respectful pastoral ministry recognizing any power imbalance within such a relationship.

Safeguarding Adults

All church workers involved in any pastoral ministry will be recruited with care including the use of the Criminal Records Bureau disclosure service when legal or appropriate. Workers will receive training and continuing support.

Any allegations of mistreatment, abuse, harassment or bullying will be responded to without delay. Whether or not the matter involves the church there will be cooperation with the police and local authority in any investigation.

Sensitive and informed pastoral care will be offered to anyone who has suffered abuse, including support to make a complaint if so desired: help to find appropriate specialist care either from the church or secular agencies will be offered.

Congregations will often include people who have offended in a way that means they are a continuing risk to vulnerable people. The risks will be managed sensitively with the protection of adults and children in mind.

The Church of England has agreed the following policy statements:

(web links are current at the time of publication)

Promoting a Safe Church (safeguarding policy for adults) 2006
https://www.churchofengland.org/clergy-office-holders/protecting-and-safeguarding-children-and-adults-who-are-vulnerable.aspx

Protecting All God's Children (safeguarding policy for children and young people, 4th edition, 2010)
https://www.churchofengland.org/media/37378/protectingallgods children.pdf

Responding to Domestic Abuse (guidelines for those with pastoral responsibility, 2006)
https://www.churchofengland.org/media/1163604/domesticabuse.pdf

Safeguarding Guidelines relating to Safer Recruitment (interim policy, 2013)
https://www.churchofengland.org/media/2097516/safer%20 recruitment%20guidance%20final%202013-6-13.pdf